MW01297828

1

Deliver Me

Whole, Healed & Free

Liz Moye Moore

First Printing: Deliver Me   Whole, Healed & Free
Copyright 2017

Author: Liz Moye Moore

Cover photography & design: Liz Moye Moore

Interior formatting: Liz Moye Moore

Editor: Tom Moore

All Scripture, unless otherwise noted, comes from the King James version of the Holy Bible

Also available in eBook form

ISBN: 13: 978-1979796682
ISBN: 10: 1979796688

Table of Contents

ACKNOWLEDGEMENTS

Faith comes by hearing and hearing by the Word of God.
Romans 10:17

For his faithfulness to stand strong on the Word of God, to teach and minister through the Holy Scripture and to lift me before the throne of God every day, I thank my precious husband and brother in Christ, Tom Moore.

FOREWORD

What is "deliverance?" What is "spiritual warfare?" Can a Christian have a demon? When Jesus hung on the cross, did He die merely for our sins? Just to pay the penalty for our sins and provide the "ticket" we needed to get us into Heaven? Or is there more? When Jesus said that He came to set the captives free and heal the broken-hearted, was He speaking only of our initial salvation experience? Or is there more? When God's Word says, "By His stripes we are healed", does this simply mean that our sins are forgiven, and we are reconciled to God? Or is there more?

Liz does a brilliant job in answering these and other questions in this step by step introductory examination of the often-veiled biblical truths of the spirit world and their operations in the life of a true believer in Christ. This book, based on the "Truth" that sets us free will give much hope to the hopeless, faith to the faithless, encouragement to the discouraged, clarity to the confused, and peace to the restless and those in turmoil.

God is sovereign! It is no accident that He has put this book into your hands. Maybe, just maybe He wants to set you free today!

Put on the whole armor of God so that you will be able to stand against all strategies and tricks of satan. For we are not fighting against people, but against "persons" without bodies (spirits)—the evil rulers of the unseen world, the huge number of those mighty satanic beings and great evil princes of darkness who rule this world (Eph. 6:11,12. TLB).

Thomas A. Moore

-- Author, teacher, minister, and most of all—a servant of the King of kings and Lord of lords... Jesus the Christ!

INTRODUCTION

I didn't recognize it at the time, but the seed of my 'experience' would be the bedrock of a productive ministry that would not come to fruition for another twenty plus years.

I was enjoying a moderately successful career in financial services when the headaches first started. I was experiencing debilitating, excruciating migraines that put me in the bed of a quiet darkened room or the hospital emergency room on a regular basis. I learned with great difficulty how to administer injections to myself to temporarily relieve the pain. I was often so blinded by the pain of the headaches, that repeated attempts to squarely land the needle in my thigh resulted in my becoming somewhat of a human pin cushion. Focusing enough to even inject myself became as difficult as the throbbing, searing pain I was already experiencing.

I recall a particularly bad episode that occurred at my office one day. One of my co-workers found me semi-conscious, huddled on the floor of a stall in the ladies' room. They had to carry me out to my car to take me home and put me in bed.

My life was equally divided between my career, ministry at the church and raising my daughter as a single (divorced) mother. I was enjoying a resurgence of my walk with Jesus after many years away from the faith. I was getting to know Him again and seeking His direction for my life. The new challenge for me was to comprehend the frequency of these migraine headaches and how to overcome the limitations created by them. I remained persistent in seeking God for healing for almost two years of these disruptions in my life. I found myself continually at church asking for prayer. One Sunday evening I met a couple there who was apparently involved in some sort of healing ministry, and they were offering prayer for me.   I jumped at the opportunity. I had nothing to lose.

The words of the prayer and the length of the prayer now seem a blur, but their dogged determination and persistence to storm the doors of heaven to obtain relief for me was clearly evident. At different points during the prolonged praying, I would even find myself thinking, "OK that's good enough." But they were relentless, and their petitions were not to be denied or delayed. And then I felt 'it' rising within me, surging from my chest through my neck and shoulders, radiating heat through my face, and a very real feeling that the top of my head just opened up and every bit of pain, tension and pressure from the headaches came rushing out. Then peace. Perfect peace. No pain. I still find words inadequate to express my experience. Still, much time would pass before I understood what 'it' was that left. I didn't know for many years what happened in the spiritual realm, but that night had been my first experience of deliverance from the powers of darkness.

Chapter 1

SEEING THE LIGHT

I married again and raised my daughter. I left the banking world and pursued other interests in women's ministry, real estate, marketing and in a few side businesses that kept me busy. Busy enough to keep me from realizing that while I had married a Christian, it was a marriage unequally yoked and we struggled to keep it together. And yes, Christians can be unequally yoked! We had each brought into our union the demons of our past sins, failures, and transgressions; and apart from a radical intercession of spiritual healing for both of us, our marriage was headed for imminent destruction. I'm not saying that our sins had not been confessed and forgiven. I'm saying that throughout our lives, we had picked up spiritual 'hitchhikers' that were settling into our soul man (mind, emotions & will); taking up residence and using every shortcoming, misstep, failure and sin to rehash, relive and make excuses for us to prevent us from ever actually walking in the freedom and healing that Christ came to give us. The understanding and teaching of these tenants is sorely neglected, even ignored in the church today. This is a mystery, especially when walking in the freedom of deliverance is the only way the Body can fully operate as outlined in the Scripture. When the powers of darkness are having their way in an individual believer's life, and those believers come together as a church, you have a church full of unclean spirits. The disjointed, powerless, unhealthy 'church' of today should be evidence enough of this fact.

My personal belief about the neglect of addressing deliverance, when it is clearly defined in Scripture, is that today's church just doesn't want to recognize or engage the spirit world. The Word of God declares in Luke 4:18, *The Spirit of the LORD is on me, because he has anointed me to proclaim good news to the poor. He has sent me to proclaim freedom for the prisoners and recovery of sight for the blind, to set the oppressed free.* It is clear from this Scripture that the primary purpose of Jesus coming to the earth, in addition to salvation, was to set the captives free and to heal the broken-hearted. And according to the very words of Jesus before He left the earth, we can use His name, His power and His authority to do the same. The typical believer today seems content to have the Holy Spirit living within them without appropriating His power. And we certainly don't want to even acknowledge the reality of the demon spirits because that's just too hocus-pocus! I find it difficult to understand why Christians don't recognize that we are a 'spirit operating in a body' rather than a 'body with a spirit.' Physical death is certainly the evidence of that! Our physical bodies WILL return to dust (Genesis 3:19). When you pass from this life to the next and breathe your last, you exhale and your spirit leaves in that breath. It goes somewhere! So why are we ignoring the most important part of our trichotomy: body, soul and spirit? The real you is your spirit, not your body!

I know there are many committed believers who will go to their graves without acknowledging that a Christian can be the residence of an evil spirit. But I would suggest that they are living in denial at the least, or sadly uneducated in the Scriptures! The Word of God states, *My people are destroyed for lack of knowledge: because thou hast rejected knowledge, I will also reject thee,* (Hosea 4:6).

Through my experiences in women's ministry, I have seen and heard the expressed 'feelings' of worthlessness, rejection, suicide, depression, anxiety and even more. They are rampant. Are you going to suggest that these 'feelings,' mental and emotional struggles come from the Holy Spirit? There is indeed a spirit moving in the church today, but it is not the one who raised our Savior from the tomb! In the Book of Revelation, John records the fall of Babylon. While we are not completely certain who Babylon represents in present day in this passage, it is clear that this is the apostate church of the last days that *'has become the habitation of devils, and the hold of every foul spirit'* (Revelation 18:2). Those evil spirits are going in where they can do the most damage – the institutional church. It is amazing to me that a believer will strongly defend their belief in the full counsel of

Scripture, only to ignore or completely delete those Bible verses that they just can't fit into their neat little man-made doctrine! There is an unjustified discomfort in many believers when dealing with the spirit world. And there is an ignorance of the knowledge of the power and authority in Christ Jesus to defeat the powers of darkness in our lives. I know I don't want to limit God in *anything* He wants for my life! I want it all.

So yes, my twenty-year marriage failed because both spouses really must want to do whatever it takes to be whole, healed, free and fully centered in Christ. People, especially believers, have a very difficult time understanding how and why Christians divorce - especially if there is an ignorance of the sovereignty of God. God sees the past, the present, and the future all at the same time. And nothing takes Him by surprise. According to the Bible, when we were in our mother's womb, God had each of our days scheduled (Psalms 139). He knew every thought, decision, every action, failure and sin before we were ever born. So, our failed marriages do not take Him by surprise. The Word of God declares: *'And we know that all things work together for good to them that love God, to them who are called according to His purpose. For whom He did foreknow, He also did* **predestinate** *to be conformed to the image of His Son, that He might be the firstborn among many brethren. Moreover, whom He did predestinate, them He also* **called***: and whom He called, them He also justified, and whom He* **justified***, them He also glorified.'* (Romans 8:28-30). So, if God **predestined, called** and **justified**, don't you think He had an idea as to how it was all going to play out? If not, then we serve a weak and powerless Creator. He certainly knew the big picture regarding the woman at the well (John 4:1-42). He knew *she had had five husbands and the one she was with was not her husband.* But He looked beyond her sins and failures because He knew she was one of His own. And because she was healed and delivered, she was used to deliver the message of forgiveness and healing! That we neglect such a perfect gospel message because we cannot understand the freedom of deliverance is such a waste of our salvation!

Chapter 2

MAKING THE CHANGE

So, I pressed into Jesus. My focus was totally redirected to pursuing joy at the feet of my Lord alone. Anything that would distract me from that singular goal was unacceptable! I moved to a neighboring state and began to re-establish my life, only this time I was following the only One who loves me completely as I am.

Shortly after settling into my new home, I gathered some things together that I no longer needed and made a trip to the local Goodwill. As I dropped off my items and pulled out to leave, I saw the sign: Refuge Ranch Ministries. I was immediately reminded of a friend who several years before had attended my church for a while. She had told me about a church that she was presently attending and the awesome move of God there. It sounded amazing, but at the time it was just too far from where I lived to be a viable option. I honestly hadn't even thought about it since then, but now God had placed me within a mile of Refuge Ranch Church (a deliverance ministry). So, I made plans to attend that Sunday. This was one of those clearly defined moments of God's sovereignty in my life! He showed up to meet me at the well that day!

Since I believe He is indeed the all-powerful Creator of the universe and has a plan for my life as His Word says, then how can anything be a mistake? Certainly, He gives us free-will. But He knows the result of our free-will choices and directs our paths within His design and those choices. And I am glad it is not all up to me!

The very next Sunday, I arrived at 'the Ranch' and was ready to hear, receive and worship. I easily found my friend who I had not seen in several years. She was delighted to see me and have an opportunity to reconnect a bit before the service. The environment was casual. The praise and worship was contemporary. Not my favorite on either point, but the room was charged with the electricity of a thunderstorm in anticipation of the release of a complete drenching of the Holy Spirit. There was no inhibition in the people to prevent them from singing, lifting their hands and dancing before the Lord. I mean REALLY dancing! They were relishing the invitation of the Lord to enter in and offer their highest praise to God! And that is what drew me in - unashamed intimacy to draw near to the Father.

When you really let the truth of the Gospel sink into your soul, how can you not respond this way?

While I was content at my current traditional church where I knew the people, and had many opportunities for ministry, I knew that 'the Ranch' ministry would have a major impact in what God had planned for my future. My friend was excited to introduce me to several people on the way out of the service, and the joy I witnessed in each of them was irrepressible. I knew instinctively that some of these people were entering my life for highly important reasons which I will later disclose.

The 'Ranch' is mainly a ministry with a church, not a church with a ministry. So, I was excited to explore the ministry aspect. The ministry, billed as 'Freed, Filled and on Fire' met on Friday nights, and I was filled with anticipation as the week moved toward that night. When you are truly seeking God with your whole heart, there are no missteps in your path to reach Him. Again, the dunamis (dynamite) power of the Holy Spirit was undeniable in the meeting place as I entered and was warmly greeted by a number of those I had met on Sunday. The praise and worship was even more dynamic, and there was a complete expectation from everyone present that God was about to do something in this place.

The ministry director, made his way to the platform. He was bold and unwavering in his declaration of God's Word. And then he began to explain the freedom in Christ of believers by appropriating the authority of Jesus in the power of the Holy Spirit to cast out demons – unclean spirits. When Jesus ordained the twelve to send them out to preach, He gave them the power to *heal sickness and CAST OUT DEMONS!* (Mark 3:15. Emphasis mine). The light of Truth illuminated my mind, and I finally saw what God had begun those 20+ years ago when the migraines left me –

DELIVERANCE!

Chapter 3

A DEMON? IN ME?

What? I'm a Christian! I was baptized – immersed even! What darkness could live in me? And yet there it was – clear evidence that something unholy was occupying my soul man. As Christians we never get to the point where we are sinless. And a Christian is an even bigger target than those who don't believe because unbelievers are not interacting with the King of the Universe – where the true power lies.

Unbelievers pose no threat to the turmoil and chaos the enemy is creating. What better 'vehicle' than a Christian for satan to occupy and work through to do his greatest damage? And Christians unknowingly open the door for the powers of darkness to come in and begin their destruction - in marriages, in families, in churches. Where ever he can get a foothold to make the Body of Christ powerless and ineffectual, satan will set up residence. Unless... we recognize his plans and stop him cold! And we have the authority and power to do just that!

No Christian will receive his total freedom and healing (mental, emotional, spiritual, physical) until he first recognizes the reality of the powers of darkness that are at work in his soul.

Fear, worry, anxiety, hopelessness, despair, depression, confusion, deception, lusts, shame, guilt, condemnation, hatred, bitterness, resentment, jealousy, quick temper, rejection, low self-worth, etc., are not just feelings or thoughts. And they are certainly not just "chemical imbalances," although that is the bill of goods that the world will try to sell you. They are unclean spirits at work in the mind, emotions, attitudes, decisions and behaviors of the unsuspecting Christian who has unknowingly become a willing participant in their designs for destruction, as well as a "vehicle" through which these wicked spirits have permission to operate.

But where does the 'demon' reside? In the body? Or outside of the body? Many, if not most Christians just can't wrap their minds around the possibility that they could house (even temporarily) a demon spirit inside of them. After all, when we get saved, the Holy Spirit comes to dwell in us-- and light and darkness cannot cohabit the same body, they would surmise. Sadly, most Pastors and "Christian Counselors" have arrived at the same conclusion.

The Word of God teaches us that we are created in the "image" of God. In other words, God is a "triune" God (Father, Son, and Holy Spirit). We also are a "trichotomy" (body, soul, and spirit). The Holy Spirit through the Apostle Paul wrote much about how as believers we are now the "temple of God" (I and II Corinthians; Ephesians), comparing us to the Old Testament Temple which had three distinct areas: the outer court, the inner court, and the "holy of holies". The outer court of the temple represents our physical bodies (our flesh). The inner court represents our souls (mind, emotion and will, i.e., our thoughts, feelings and decisions). The most inward part of the temple, the Holy of Holies, represents our spirits- the real person! The real you!

When we confess our sins to God, repenting of them, asking God for forgiveness based upon the finished work of Jesus on the cross, asking Jesus to come live in us, and receiving His gift of eternal life… the Holy Spirit comes to dwell in our SPIRIT man—the "holy of holies!" No demon can ever intrude or invade that sacred space where "Christ dwells in our hearts!" No entity of darkness can cohabit that special place where the "Light of the World" has taken up residence! Satan himself cannot touch our spirit man. We are eternally secured and preserved from the powers of darkness!

However, the Apostle Paul also addresses the areas of our lives where we give satan permission or the "legal right" to enter our bodies and souls (II Corinthians 10:4). These are called "strongholds" or "holds", meaning "bondages." (Revelation 18:2). God's Word says that as believers we can potentially allow unclean spirits to have a powerful influence or "stronghold" in our minds. So, let me ask you, where is the mind located? Is it outside the body? Or is it inside the body? The answer is a no-brainer. The physical brain and the spiritual mind are *inside* the body. And

THAT, Paul tells us is where the unclean powers of darkness reside to do their ugly work of destruction in and through that person. Satan knows he must first gain access into a Christian's mind in order to control that person's attitudes, thoughts, emotions, decisions and behaviors. He knows that the brain or mind is the "central control center" of the personality and temperament of that individual. So, he assigns demons of destruction to enter the mind, in order to control the person. This is exactly why Peter admonishes us to "gird up the loins of your mind!" And Paul instructs us to "put on the helmet of salvation." (Ephesians 6:17; I Thessalonians 5:8). It may be a shock to many Christians that they not only carry in their bodies the Holy Spirit of Truth, but their bodies are also vehicles of several (if not many) wicked spirits of satan's kingdom.

Can a Christian be "possessed" by a demon? The word "possession" in the Greek language denotes the idea of "total ownership." We who belong to

Christ, having been born-again, are totally and exclusively the possession of Christ. We are His "treasured possession!" So, NO! We cannot be "owned" by satan.

But the secondary meaning of that Greek word denotes: "to come under the influence of something else, or someone else; to be influenced or altered by an outside source or entity." Therefore, a true born-again Christian *can* have a demon (or many demons) working in his soul (mind, emotions and will); but he will never have a demon in his spirit! This is precisely why Christian Counseling that is short of "deliverance" does not work. This is also why prescribed; mind-altering drugs do not work. The demons are still in the soul man, operating according to the will and power of satan. They are trespassers! They must be evicted! They must be kicked out of the soul and body by the power and authority of Jesus! This is what Jesus did in over two-thirds of His ministry. And this is what He commanded us to do! This is what He empowered and authorized us to do!

Pay attention to this powerful verse of Scripture:

Haven't you yet learned that your body (and soul and spirit) is the temple of God the Holy Spirit, who lives in you? Your own body does not belong to you (you do not own or possess it, and neither should satan). For God has bought you with a great price (the death of His Own Son). So, use every part of your body (and soul and spirit) to give glory back to God, because HE OWNS IT! (I Corinthians. 6: 19, 20...TLB).

I don't know about you, but I don't want anything inside of me except the Holy Spirit of Truth and Purity! Nothing and no one residing in me except my Lord and Savior Jesus Christ!

Chapter 4

THE UNDERSTANDING

I had been delivered from the headaches. But more relevant was understanding the underlying cause of them. The headaches were merely symptoms of the root causes that were driven by unclean spirits that I unknowingly and ignorantly invited into my mind through my own sins and/or generational curses (the sins of my ancestors). As a born-again believer there were seasons in my life when I lived in rebellion against God, opening the doors for the powers of darkness to come in and inflict immense pain in my body to render me incapacitated in my spiritual walk with Christ. In short, my disobedience gave unclean spirits the legal right to inflict physical pain in my body.

We must first understand that it is an unclean spirit that we often allow to come in to our soul that manipulates our thinking, emotions, and behavior, as a result of our rejection by someone we love. We fall in love. Our beloved spurns us for another. We are of course wounded. If we do not go to Jehovah Rapha (the God Who Heals) to heal our deepest hurts and wounds, and if we do not forgive those who have hurt and wounded us, then the tormenting spirit of rejection will enter our mind, emotions and will and wreak havoc in our lives. It is the lying voice that says, "you are not loved". If we do not shut down that voice and cast it out in the name of Jesus, then the unclean spirits will whisper "you are unworthy". Oh, my gracious! So, we just assume the lies of the enemy to be true rather than recognize them as the voice of the one who seeks to kill and destroy. Since we know these spirits are not the fruit of the Spirit (*love, joy, peace, patience, kindness, goodness, faithfulness, gentleness,* and *self-control* Galatians 5:22), they have to be unclean spirits.

When you receive that message of rejection and unworthiness, self-doubt and self-pity come in and set up house. You are now loading up your vehicle (self) with 'hitchhikers' (unclean spirits) and don't even recognize it. You feel bad about feeling bad. You begin to blame yourself or someone else. And self-blame is joined by his friends: rejection, self-loathing, despair, depression, hopelessness, guilt, and self-condemnation. This now becomes your normal way of living. But it doesn't have to be!

In my case, I had no clue that these were unclean spirits working in my mind, emotions and will. These unclean spirits manifested themselves as migraine headaches with the goal of rendering me ineffectual and powerless in the kingdom of God! Once the 'hitchhikers' were cast out, the headaches ceased. But that did not resolve all my issues because they were still many other spirits that needed to be evicted. Sadly, it was many years before I was to be freed from all the 'stuff' I was hauling around!

Some of the ways the unclean spirits manifested came in the form of depression and anxiety. Responding like every other patient complaining of these symptoms, I just medicated them with prescription drugs. The medications had a numbing and hypnotic effect on my brain, but they didn't resolve the root cause. So Christian counseling was my next choice of treatment. Even in Christian counseling, there is seldom teaching of identifying and evicting these 'trespassers.' And my well-meaning counselors just upped my meds. However, these attempts to resolve my issues gave me none of the freedom and peace that I received when those demons were rebuked in Jesus name because —

YOU CAN'T MEDICATE OR COUNSEL DEMONS!

They *want* to stay in there. They *want* to destroy you. They are not your friends. So how do we understand exactly who the 'hitchhikers' are, what is their goal or assignments in our lives, and how do we get them out?

There are typically four areas in our lives that demons use as entry points into the soul: bitterness or unforgiveness toward those who have hurt us, soul-ties, the occult, and generational/ancestral curses. My husband and I regularly facilitate deliverance and ask our clients to thoroughly examine each of these areas. The process of delving into these four areas should be exhaustive, but also worthwhile to accomplish. Jesus frequently expelled demons prior to healing. So indeed, the potential for healing is there when demons have been expelled. In the last chapter of this book, I will walk you through a self-examination, so you can begin the process of taking yourself through deliverance.

Luke, the Physician, spoke frequently about the healings Jesus performed after casting out demons. I love that Luke recognized the source of illness was not always treated with medication! Sadly, in our world today most Physicians fail to recognize any spiritual implications of their patient's illnesses. Even those in medical practice with the best intentions operate from a 'let's put a bandage on it' mentality. In most cases, pharmaceuticals are often the first course of treatment. Something that you may find interesting as you begin to understand deliverance is that the origin of the word pharmaceutical is from the Greek 'pharmakia' which means 'witchcraft'. The word witchcraft in the Scriptures denotes control, manipulation, domination and intimidation. In short, many in the medical industry unintentionally and unknowingly align themselves with the powers of darkness! Doesn't that give you pause before you fill that next prescription?

Prior to going through deliverance, I was taking about 12 prescriptions for everything from pain to anxiety and depression. Now? None. The unclean spirits that caused those manifestations are gone! For the past 25 years since my initial deliverance I have not had a single migraine headache! Praise God!

I know that for whatever reason God does not choose to heal all illnesses and diseases. But shouldn't you go to Him first?

My husband's father, a Pastor and godly man went through a life-threatening bout with melanoma. The Specialists at

Duke University Medical Center told him he had 6-9 months to live. God supernaturally healed him, and he lived another healthy and productive 17 years. Another form of cancer came, and his earthly life came to an end. But praise God, he received his ultimate healing by leaving his temporal earthly body and entering in to his glorious eternal 'body' with Jesus!

Last year, my husband was diagnosed with melanoma. The surgeons found 4 places on his body that they wanted to excise and treat. The doctors strongly encouraged him to schedule a surgery in order to get the cancer out! But after much prayer and believing God's promise to *heal all thy diseases* (Psalms 103:3), we chose against the surgeon's recommendation. My husband was healed by God without the expense and invasive measures of a surgical procedure. My point is, if we do not appropriate God's Word in ALL things, aren't we missing out of the very best He has to offer? I mean really, shouldn't we consider that cancer is just another invasive demon? It will always be a mystery why God in His sovereign plan chooses to heal some and not others. But if I err, I will always 'err' on the side of believing God's promises-- not man's prognosis!

Let's take a closer look at who the demonic spirits are and the impact they have on our lives.

Chapter 5

DEEPEST HURTS, WOUNDS & BETRAYALS

The very first area or entry point for a demon to enter our lives is through our own bitterness, unforgiveness and resentment toward those who have deeply hurt us, wounded us, or betrayed us. Jesus said, *if you do not forgive those who have offended you, the tormentors will be sent to you and torment you day and night* (Matthew 18: 35). In this teaching of Jesus, He is obviously telling us that through our unforgiveness towards others we are inviting unclean spirits into our lives.

It is critical to examine our deepest hurts, wounds and betrayals. It is helpful to write them down on paper. This can be a lengthy process, but this way we can determine if we have forgiven our trespassers. If you saw your 'offender' in the mall, would your reaction be to head in the other direction? If so, there is probably some unforgiveness in your heart.

Typically, the list starts with our parents. Even in the very best of homes, parents are operating from their own hurts, wounds, betrayals and limitations. We must acknowledge their humanity and fallen nature. Forgive them and bless them and ask God to bless them if they are still living. Make your list. You will no doubt continue adding to it as the Holy Spirit brings people to your mind. Don't forget your siblings, relatives, childhood friends, teachers, employers, romantic interests and ex-spouses.

I remember when I was in the sixth grade, my mother worked at a potato chip plant. Each Christmas season, the company gave out a generous supply of chips, crackers and nuts to their employees. My mother gave me several snacks to take to school to share with my friends at recess. I was so excited to share but imagine my disappointment when all my so-called friends came and took all my treats and ran off together to enjoy them, leaving me standing there empty handed and alone. As a child, how do we process that kind of disappointment and rejection? We stuff it down in our 'vehicle' where it becomes another 'hitchhiker' that will continue the lie - 'No one likes you; you are unworthy.' You no doubt have some similar stories of your own. Haven't you carried those hurts and wounds for long enough?

Speak aloud their names to God and call out the transgression(s). "Lord Jesus, I repent of the sin of unforgiveness, bitterness and resentment. I forgive my sixth-grade classmates for using and rejecting me. Lord, I ask You to forgive them and bless them in Jesus' name!" When you do that, something happens in the spirit world. Demons scatter! As long as the demons have your permission to continue to regurgitate all the meanness from the people who treated you so poorly, you are giving them the go ahead to continue their abuse in you. When you shine light on them and on the sin of unforgiveness, the unclean spirits all scatter like cockroaches! I will cover the steps more fully in Chapter 10.

Don't think any trespass is too small. If you are still remembering it even 50 years later, you are walking in unforgiveness and Scripture clearly says don't do it! After all, you want to be able to receive forgiveness when you come to your Heavenly Father: *If you do not forgive others, neither will your Father who is in heaven forgive your trespasses.* (Mark 11:26).

Chapter 6

SOUL-TIES

A soul tie is usually an unholy physical or sexual relationship outside of a God-ordained marriage. Sexual immorality is so socially acceptable these days it's often ignored. But if you are a believer, don't be deceived on this issue. If you have lived in sexual sin in the past or are presently living in sexual immorality, you have opened wide the door to the powers of darkness. You need to address it pronto! Any intimate sexual relationship potentially offers the opportunity for the powers of darkness to enter in to your body and soul. Therefore, it is vitally important for both you and your potential marriage partner to go through deliverance prior to coming together in marriage. Sexual assault or molestation also creates a soul tie. Many men and women who were sexually assaulted as children unknowingly were invaded by an unclean spirit which eventually causes them to practice homosexuality as an adult. The Bible declares in 1 Corinthians 6:18 that sexual sin (regardless of cause) is a *sin against your body*. If you experienced any sort of molestation, those demons from your perpetrator set up residence in you! You MUST expel them!! And in instances such as these, you must also forgive the offender! There are usually several 'trespassing spirits' that enter the bodies of victims of sexual molestation. This is an example of satan pulling a double or triple whammy. Let's say you were sexually molested. Now you not only have forgiveness and soul ties to address, but all the other unclean spirits that were transferred to you from the perpetrator. (Genesis 6 - the transference of demons from the Anakin and Nephilim into the bodies of women through sexual intercourse).

I know of an instance where a familial satanic ritual involved sexual molestation. In this situation, the one seeking deliverance had to address the generational curses as well as the occult spirits. The point I'm trying to make here is to not leave any stone unturned. Remember, when you turn a stone over, there is usually vermin crawling underneath! Unclean spirits like to work in groups - where there is one, there are more.

Soul-ties are not restricted only to a physical or sexual nature. Any deeply, intense, unholy relationship tie where Christ is not honored needs to be broken as well. These can include business relationships where one or more partners is not a Christian and/or is not practicing Biblical principles. The same for close sibling ties, friendships, and even unequally yoked marital ties. When soul-ties are broken, you uncover new ground for establishing holy Christ-honoring intimate relationships.

Chapter 7

GENERATIONAL & ANCESTRAL CURSES

Exodus 34:7 clearly addresses generational curses. The Word of God speaks of *visiting the iniquity of the fathers upon the children, and upon the children's children unto the third and the fourth generation.* What do you think that means if not that we will receive some repercussion from the sins of our fathers? After all, Adam was our father! This is pretty clear, but for some reason we relegate the reality of this revelation to a 'doesn't apply to me ' status.

I have a friend whose father was an alcoholic. Her mother was addicted to prescription medication as well as alcohol. My friend sought deliverance from the powers and effects of these generational curses of addictions. Today, my friend is walking in freedom. Anytime those old spirits try to revisit, she now knows she has the power in Jesus' name to rebuke them and cast them out. Sadly, her siblings remain in prison at various stages of addiction from functioning alcoholism to just straight up drunks. Even now there is evidence that my friend's nieces and nephews are taking up the mantle of addictions. This is one of many examples of generational curses.

My friend's parents were also serial adulterers with multiple marriages. This was also the case with my friend and her siblings. But after breaking those generational curses, and evicting those wicked spirits working through those curses, my friend is now in a solid Christ-honoring marriage!

There are many types of generational and ancestral curses. I was delighted when I found out I could trace my heritage to George Washington. But understanding his involvement in the Free Masons created the issue of a generational curse I needed to break. While Free Masonry presents itself as a philanthropic organization, at its very core the 'god' of Freemasonry is not the God of the Holy Scriptures. They serve a false god. Now, I certainly don't want that curse imputed to me!

This isn't to create an attitude of despair, but rather the hope and the promise that by *His stripes we ARE healed!* (*Isaiah* 53:5). We just need to learn how to appropriate the healing our Lord has already provided.

We love our native American friends, but the 'god' of the wind, the river, or the 'great spirit' is not the Holy Father, Yahweh. Therefore, if you can trace any of your heritage to the American Indian, the curse of pantheism (worshiping creation and not the Creator) needs to be broken from your life. *Thou shall have no other gods before me.* (Exodus 20:36). Another generational curse may involve false teaching and false religions such as Mormonism, Jehovah's false Witnesses, Hinduism, Islam, or the New Age Movement which says there are many ways to get to God (Jesus said: "I am the only Way; I am the only Truth!"). So, explore your heritage as best you can and cast out those unclean spirits and break those generational curses off of you and your children.

Generational/Ancestral curses run the gamut. Physical illness, mental illnesses, immoral behavior, occultism, addictions, etcetera, are just a few examples. Very few of us have all the information or knowledge of the personal lives of even our most recent ancestors. Most people living before the 1950's actually lived in a cloak of secrecy. Today, for better or worse, everyone likes to parade their sin down main street. Isaiah 3:9 states the same thing; *The look on their faces testifies against them; they parade their sin like Sodom; they do not hide it. Woe to them! They have brought disaster upon themselves.* (NIV)

It does, however, give us the opportunity to identify what we are dealing with, so we can kick it to the curb!

Remember, Jesus became a curse for us (Galatians 3:13). But we still must appropriate everything He did for us on the cross.

Chapter 8

THE OCCULT

It seems that the occult would be one of the most obvious but is often the least understood. Because satan is the deceiver and because Christians cannot wrap their minds around the spirit world, they envision the occult as a red devil with horns and a cape. They are deceived!

In our practice of deliverance, we have run into only one person who had no obvious evidence of the occult in his life.

And most don't think they do. They see it as innocent fun, but again – deception.

In elementary school, my girlfriends and I used to have sleepovers where we played with the Ouija board and had séances. We were playing, but do not assume for a minute that those demons didn't rush in to infiltrate the innocence of six young girls. One of those girls, my childhood friend now in her 60s is a full-fledged tarot card reading, palm reading, astrologer practicing witchcraft!

'Well, I don't do that' you might say. But, have you ever had your palm read? Have you ever read your horoscope? Participated in Halloween? Had your fortune told? Played the game, 'Dungeons and Dragons?' Practiced Yoga? My friend, these are the doors satan uses to let the spirits of darkness and evil to enter your soul man.

Let's consider abortion. For many, it is just a matter of an individual or political choice. However, the evil practice of child sacrifice to the demon god Molech was a common practice in the Old Testament – but was totally forbidden by God. What is abortion but child sacrifice? The sacrifice of children through abortion for convenience sake is just another occultic practice which invites the spirit of murder into the lives of the ones who participate in the sin of abortion. Do not be deceived! You are playing with Hell-fire. Cast those demons out and bolt the door!

Chapter 9

STILL DOUBTING?

I recently heard a testimony from a friend who is a godly woman, deeply in love with Jesus. She had been working on a two-year ministry commitment and it had been a spiritual struggle for the entire time. She was under attack. She sobbed as she shared her feelings of utter hopelessness and unworthiness, and how it would be better if she could just end it all. She said she often thought about just driving her car off the road and into a tree just to be free of the pain.

Suicide is another unclean spirit that works with the spirits of hopelessness, despair, low self-worth, depression and rejection. And as I said before, these spirits are like gangs. They run in groups. If you are still doubting that satan is alive and well in this world and out to destroy the children of the Most High, we need to have a face to face conversation! Where do you think that kind of desperation comes from? As the 'church lady' would say, "Could it be…. Satan?" (SNL). And she would be right. What I know is that my friend is harboring unclean spirits that will not let up on her until they destroy her, or she is delivered! Oh, they will settle down, but unless they are evicted they will look for the opportune moment to reappear.

As far as deliverance goes, this is just the tip of the iceberg. There are as many demons as there are sins to manifest them.

Deepest hurts, wounds and betrayals, soul-ties, generational curses, the occult

- these are critical starting points in your freedom through deliverance. Any sin in your life is a foothold for the enemy to come in and hitch a ride. As I said, if it has been confessed, it is forgiven and under the blood of Jesus. But that will not stop the enemy from digging in with guilt and accusations. Remember, *Satan is the accuser of the brethren* (Revelation 12:10). And *Now the Spirit speaketh expressly, that in the latter times some shall depart from the faith, giving heed to seducing spirits ...* (1 Timothy 4). So, GET THEM OUT!

It is a lot of work, you bet! But oh, how blessed is the freedom when you are driving a clean vehicle. You know how your car seems to drive better after you take it through the carwash? Imagine how great it will run if you get it tuned up and put new clean oil in it?

Deliverance must become a way of life because those demons are not going to give up so easily. Each time those demons whisper that you are a failure, unloved, worthless, etc., you must again rebuke them in the name of Jesus and command them to leave. When you are tempted to sin, these same demons will whisper," It's OK! No one will know." It's a lie from the pit of hell and smells like smoke.

Whoever said walking the Christian life would be easy wasn't a Christian! It may be the hardest and most difficult thing you will ever do. But the reward of walking in and with the Spirit of God is immeasurable by any standard. And the overwhelming peace and joy that comes with deliverance is certainly worth the effort!

Remember when I told you about the people I met that came into my life for highly important reasons? Well, that would be the man that God called alongside me to minister with - my husband, Tom Moore! After my divorce, I was content to be alone with Jesus, but God had other plans. That is how our sovereign God works! Now, Tom and I are in ministry together, writing and sharing the good news of deliverance. I could have never created so perfect a scenario, but God....

Chapter 10

THE STEPS TO DELIVERANCE

Hopefully you have a better understanding of deliverance and the many benefits to making the life changing effort to fully realize what freedom Christ has for you. I am going to give you some simple steps to help direct you toward beginning your deliverance.

As I mentioned in Chapter 5, it is imperative to begin with forgiveness. On a sheet of paper, write down the names of everyone you can recall who has hurt, wounded or betrayed you. (You will also be completing similar lists for the other categories; soul-ties, occult and generational curses). Since you are doing this on your own, it is not necessary to write down the offense, as you will remember it as soon as their name is spoken.   Starting with the first person on your list say, "I forgive _____(person) for _____ (name the offense), and I ask You, my Heavenly Father to forgive them and bless them in Jesus' name. In the name of Jesus, I bind every unclean spirit of unforgiveness, bitterness, resentment and anger toward all of my offenders. I have forgiven them all. All tormenting spirits must come out of me now. Leave in Jesus' name!"

That's it! So simple! And that is how you start. Speak out loud! It is important that satan hears you forgiving your offenders. This takes away his power. As you go down the list, depending on the depth of the wound, you may experience deep sorrow, grief, tears, even anger. That is okay, because when you go through the process, it most likely will be the last time you feel that way. I say, 'most likely' because there may be external forces that recreate or cause you to remember the transgression in the future. When that happens, immediately restate (aloud) your forgiveness statement. Complete your list. This is typically the biggest part of your deliverance and you may begin to feel lighter – emotionally and physically. Some clients have said it almost felt like they lost weight! Of course, we know the weight they are losing is the weight of the burden of unforgiveness and the unclean spirits associated with it.

Next you will tackle soul-ties. This time you are not only going to forgive those who violated you, but you are going to ask God to forgive you for your role in the commission of the sin. Say, "Lord, please forgive my sin of _____ (name the offense). I forgive_____ (name the person) for_____ (name the offense). And I ask You to forgive them. And in Jesus' name, I break all soul ties that I made with _____ (name the person). I break these soul ties mentally, emotionally, spiritually, physically and sexually. I now take authority, in Jesus' name over every wicked spirit including sexually perverted spirits that I invited into my soul through my soul ties. I have confessed my sins and broken all soul ties. You must leave me now in Jesus' name."

When you tackle the <u>Occult</u>, it is important that you recognize the demonic nature of the occult. It is helpful to quote Scripture regarding God's opinion of the occult.

*And the soul that turneth after such as have **familiar spirits**, and after **wizards**, to go a whoring after them, **I will even set my face against that soul, and will cut him off from among his people.*** (Leviticus 20:6).   That is a pretty clear directive regarding the offense! You do not want to be cut off from God!

Here is an occultic offense that is rarely recognized – *For rebellion [is as] the sin of **witchcraft**...* (1 Samuel 15:23). Who could ever say they did not practice rebellion in some form? Thus, we have all been guilty of some form of witchcraft at some point in our life

And if you think you have cleared the test, consider Paul's question to the Galatians:

*O foolish Galatians, who hath **bewitched** you, that ye should not obey the truth, before whose eyes Jesus Christ hath been evidently set forth, crucified among you?* (Galatians 3:1).

So, working with your list, confess aloud: "Father, forgive me for practicing _____ (name the offense). I ask you to cleanse me and restore me from all my unrighteousness. I realize now that I had invited unclean spirits into my soul by participating in the occult. In the name of Jesus, I take authority over every wicked spirit that I have invited in through my participation in the occult. I bind you, render you powerless and inoperative in my life. I now command you, in Jesus' name to come out of my soul and leave me now."

Generational/Ancestral curses are typically not something of which you are aware. We are not necessarily a participant in the sins of our fathers and mothers before us. However, since we are born with a sin nature and under the curse of Adam, we want to clear any possibility that there are any malingering unclean spirits. Working down your list, speak aloud, "Father, I break the generational curses on my life of:

- Alcoholism, drugs and all other addictions
- Sexual perversion (adultery, fornication, molestation, homosexuality, etc.).
- Depression and anxiety
- Fear
- Rejection
- Low self-esteem, low self-worth, self-pity
- Anger, rage, quick temper
- Rebellion
- Occult - satanism, witchcraft, freemasonry
- Physical and mental illnesses

I don't want the sins of my fathers and mothers before me to affect my life.

Therefore, in Jesus' name, I break all generational/ancestral curses off my life right now. And in the name of Jesus, I break and cancel all the assignments of the powers of darkness that work through these generational curses. I command you evil spirits to come out of my soul and leave my body now, in Jesus' name."

Chapter 11

DID YOU MISS ONE?

I hope I have given you enough information to help you identify the unclean spirits that will try to come into your life, so you can recognize them when they show up. Below is a sample list of wicked spirits. This is not an exhaustive list by any means but hopefully will help you discern these predators. Remember, these spirits can and will trigger emotional and physical responses. But those are the symptoms and not the root cause! The causes are demonic spirits that have assignments to kill, steal and destroy you! A number of these will fall into more than one category so identify which 'major' spirit you are dealing with. I have placed an asterisk by some of the ones we have addressed in this book.

FEAR: of man, of the future, of poverty, of illness, of dying, of divorce, etc.

WORRY: anxiety*, insecurity, distrust of God and/or man, doubt, unbelief

ADDICTIONS: sex*, money, materialism, drugs*, alcohol*, pornography

IDOLATRY: greed, materialism, entertainment, self

SEXUAL PERVERSION: pornography, adultery*, lust of the eyes, mind and flesh, homosexuality, lesbianism, bestiality, fornication

ANGER: wrath, rage, quick temper, revenge

WITCHCRAFT*: control, manipulation, domination, intimidation

SELF: centeredness, pity, importance, false humility

REJECTION*: low self-esteem, worthlessness

PRIDE: haughty, arrogance, boasting, conceit, self-promotion

REBELLION: self-aggrandizement

RESENTMENT: bitterness, unforgiveness, hatred

LYING: deceit, deception

STEALING: theft, embezzlement, plagiarism

RELIGION*: holier than thou, self-righteousness, pride, man-made traditions

MENTAL ILLNESS*: anxiety, depression, bi-polar, schizophrenia

PHYSICAL ILLNESS*: cancer, high blood pressure, migraine headaches, diabetes, etc.

So, I think you get the idea. Anything that is not of God is of satan - and you don't want anything to do with him! When you read through this list you may identify more strongholds that you want to address. Make another list and address those issues in the same way we outlined in Chapter 10.

In Luke 4:18, Jesus quoted Isaiah saying: *The Spirit of the Lord is upon me, because he hath anointed me to preach the gospel to the poor; he hath sent me to heal the brokenhearted, to preach* **deliverance** *to the captives, and recovering of sight to the blind, to set at liberty them that are bruised.*

Are you **poor** in spirit? **Brokenhearted** by your frailty? **Captive** by demons of your past or present? **Blind** to all Jesus has for you? Then now is your time for deliverance!   Now is your time for freedom! Embrace the gospel, the good news! Be healed and delivered in Jesus' name.   Appropriate the salvation, deliverance and freedom that is yours through the blood of the Lamb.

FINAL THOUGHTS

Had I not been on this journey and experienced the amazing freedom of deliverance, I would not have the passion and urgency to share this good news with you. If you have questions and want more information about deliverance, please do not hesitate to contact me. Our personal emails are:

tommooreconnects@gmail.com

onemoyegirl@gmail.com

My husband Tom and I have been privileged to be used by God to 'set the captives free and heal the broken hearted.' And we want to see you Freed, Filled and on Fire!

For further study on the subject of Deliverance

Spiritual Warfare, Derek Prince

Protection from Deception, Derek Prince

Satan's Greatest Weapon: The Deception of Religion, Thomas A. Moore

Satan's Greatest Weapon Part II: The Deception of Idolatry, Thomas A. Moore

Satan's Greatest Weapon Part III: The Deception of Ignorance, Thomas A. Moore

Deliverance Ministries

Refuge Ranch Ministries
www.refugeranch.info

About the Author

Liz Moye Moore was born and raised in Atlanta, Georgia. She attended Reinhardt University and spent her professional career in the financial services industry. Now retired, she and her husband Tom spend their days writing and ministering the good news of deliverance.

Made in the USA
Middletown, DE
03 December 2018